HOW SECOND-PLACE LEADERS LEAD

"Leading Others for Others"

LANDERS B. HARDY

LANDERS B. HARDY
Global Profits Education
21478 Osprey Woods Cir
Orlando, Florida 32820
407-595-2447
landers@freshapproach.biz

Fresh Approach Consulting
www.globalprofeds.com

Printed in the United States of America
First Printing 2023
First Edition 2023

ISBN: 979-8-9859713-4-7

HOW SECOND-PLACE LEADERS LEAD

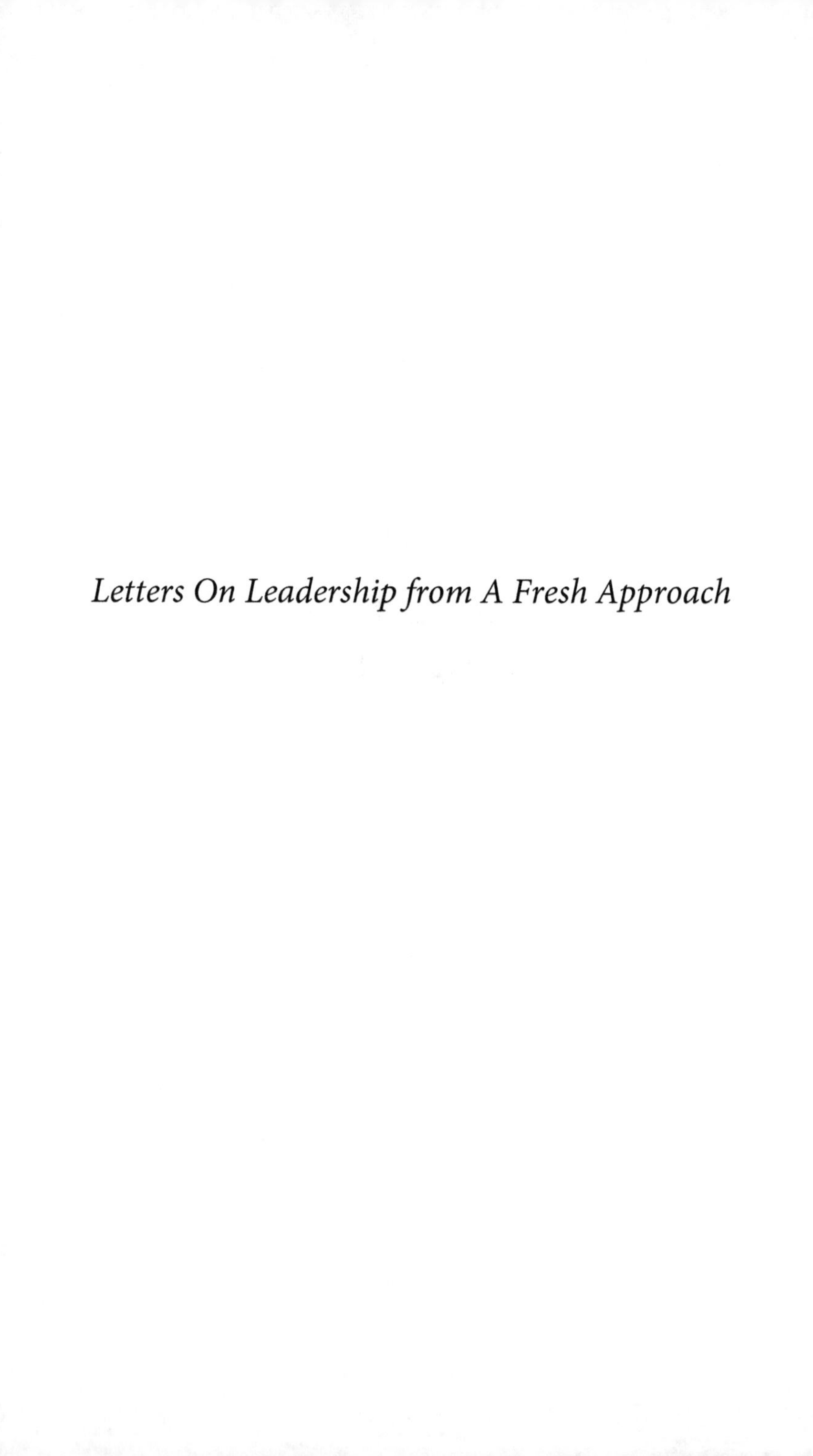

Letters On Leadership from A Fresh Approach

DEDICATION

This book is a heartfelt tribute to my beloved father, James Moses Hardy, who has now joined the embrace of the Lord. Within these pages, I seek to honor the man to whom I owe not only my early lessons in leadership and entrepreneurship but also the enduring love and cherished memories that have shaped my life.

Dad, you were more than a parent – you were my guiding light, my first mentor, and an unwavering source of inspiration. As I reflect on my journey, I am reminded of the countless moments we shared, from the age of 12 and throughout my formative years up to the halls of my first year in community college. Your willingness to let me accompany you on your business ventures granted me an invaluable education that extended beyond books and classrooms.

Even while your expertise as a serial entrepreneur was apparent, your legacy, Dad, went beyond just being one of entrepreneurial ability. Additionally, it was a legacy of kindness, determination, and the capacity to remain composed in the face of difficulties. Your composure helped me navigate life's challenges like a lighthouse in crazy waters.

I am fully aware that, as I write down my thoughts and experiences, I am documenting not just my personal path but also the echoes of your knowledge that have been woven into the very fiber of who I am. You gave me the will to endure, the ambition to lead, and the heart to look for meaning in whatever I do.

Though you may no longer walk by my side, your presence remains palpable in every step I take, every decision I make, and every accomplishment I achieve. This book is a testament to the lasting impact you've had on my life, and I hope to pass on the torch of your teachings to future generations.

Dad, as I share these pages with the world, I do so with profound gratitude for the love, guidance, and enduring lessons you have bestowed upon me. You are not just a chapter in my life – you are the very essence that runs through each page of my journey.

With heartfelt affection and a deep sense of Dedication.

Landers B. Hardy

TABLE OF CONTENTS

FOREWORD

By Bishop Allen TD Wiggins

Leadership is often regarded as a privilege and a responsibility, but it is also undeniably a "mindset." To inspire others to passionately pursue a vision articulated by their leader and to embrace that vision as their own requires a unique blend of influence, encouragement, meticulous planning, and, above all, the power of persuasive communication. Much like the intricate workings of a well-oiled machine, achieving this synergy necessitates a substantial investment of influence, encouragement, planning, and a whole lot of "pep talk." Any great leader will undoubtedly acknowledge that their remarkable achievements would have remained elusive and unfulfilled without the invaluable support of an exceptional team.

Before a team can execute a plan with maximum efficiency, someone must focus on the minutiae to ensure it functions like a precisely calibrated instrument. Often, this role falls to someone operating discreetly in the shadow of the primary leader—the Second-Place Leader.

I've had the privilege of observing Landers Hardy excel in various domains, be it in business, ministry, or family. In each arena, he naturally assumes the posture of a leader, driven by a deep desire to see others reach their God-given potential. His ultimate satisfaction lies in helping others realize their purpose and achieve their dreams.

Drawing from his diverse life experiences, Landers Hardy has authored "The Second Place Leader." This book serves as a valuable resource for those who are frequently overlooked and left to fend for themselves. Landers has attained a set of skills that make him highly proficient in managing emotions, responsibilities, purpose, and team execution. Throughout the pages of this book, Landers shares compelling testimonials that can serve as real-life case studies, fostering corporate empathy and enlightenment. It extends its support to every member of the team, including those positioned at the very top.

Landers poses thought-provoking questions and provides candid answers that can revolutionize one's mindset. If anyone possesses the credentials, experience, insight, and battle scars to deliver life-changing messages, it's Landers Hardy. This book will inspire and motivate builders, bring healing to the wounded, and accelerate the realization of visions for all who delve into its profound content.

The title of the book, "Second Place Leader," in itself is both eye-opening and revelatory. It compels us to pause and appreciate those who have sacrificed so much for the sake of our collective success. What remarkable gifts our Father has bestowed upon us to ensure His divine vision is fulfilled! As Jesus stated, "I have glorified You on the earth. I have finished the work which You have given Me to do" (John 17:4 NKJV). With humility, we come to understand that all our accomplishments are divinely ordained to magnify our Creator. In this context, second place becomes the winning position in the Kingdom race.

Archbishop Allen T.D. Wiggins

Presiding Prelate, The International Bishops Conference, Inc. USA - ibishop.org, Senior Pastor, The Hope Church of Orlando - thehopechurch.org, Founder, Hope Center West - A live, work, learn, play, and worship community ecosystem. The first half of the two-time Stellar Award-Winning Inspirational Jazz Duo, Allen & Allen Author, "Daily Hope: A 40 Day Devotional to Ignite Hope in Times of Despair" - shop.bishopatdw.com

INTRODUCTION

As I look back over my 41 years as a leader in different positions throughout my adult life, I've come to realize that there are numerous books written about leadership. However, I've noticed a lack of focus on the leaders who support the top leader. We've all heard of these roles - vice presidents, assistant coaches, assistant district attorneys, assistant pastors, and more. These positions are crucial to the success of the top leader and the organization. They can be challenging; however, they play a key role in helping the top leader achieve his or her vision, dreams, and goals. I entitled this role "The Second-Place Leader."

Many individuals in these positions are ambitious themselves. They have their own visions, dreams, and goals. While some may genuinely prefer supporting others, many probably aspired to be in the top position themselves. This book seeks to discuss what it means to be second in command, responsible for someone else's vision, goals, and dreams, and how to effectively lead others for others.

Throughout my professional career, I have predominantly operated in the role of second in command, providing me with valuable experience and insight into this topic. My journey began as a young teenager when I was thrust into supervising a few of my father's employees in his businesses. My father's leadership and guidance inspired me to support him in his ventures, fostering a desire to assist him in his businesses.

In the military, I received formal training as a leader, and over the years of service, I attended numerous leadership development courses. No matter how high I climbed in the ranks, I always had someone else to report to, (DON'T WE ALL) teaching me the importance of supporting the dreams and goals of others while pursuing my own ambitions.

John Maxwell's quote from "Developing Leaders Around You" resonates with me: "Those closest to the leader will determine the success level of that leader." Effective leaders by the leader's side are vital for achieving greatness. As the second in command, I quickly learned the importance of developing strong leaders within the organization to aid in its success.

Throughout this book, I want to encourage Second-Place Leaders to examine how they carry out their duties and responsibilities. Supporting your leader wholeheartedly, functioning at your best, avoiding ambition-driven actions, developing others around you, and sowing positive seeds of leadership are essential elements to excel in this role. By the end of this book, I hope you gain a deeper understanding of what it means to lead for others and stay focused and supportive while working toward shared goals.

CHAPTER I

UNDERSTANDING LEADERSHIP

Leadership is an art, a science, and a responsibility that carries immense influence over the lives of others. John Maxwell says, "Leadership is influence, nothing more, nothing less. The traditional notion of leadership often revolves around the image of an individual standing tall on a pedestal, commanding the troops, and basking in the glory of their achievements. However, this singular focus on personal success can be limiting and shortsighted.

Enter the concept of the "Second-Place Leader." The term might sound peculiar at first, but its essence lies in the profound impact it can have on the lives of those being led. A Second-Place Leader is someone who rises above the ego-driven pursuit of first place and instead embraces the noble journey of leading others for others.

True leadership transcends self-interest and centers on the collective well-being of the team, organization, or community. It involves putting the needs and aspirations of others before one's own, fostering an environment of trust, empathy, and growth. But how do we truly understand and embody this kind of leadership?

At its core, leadership involves guiding and inspiring others to achieve a common goal. Effective leaders possess a blend of qualities that set them apart from the rest. Charisma, decisiveness, and vision are often touted as essential leadership traits. While these attributes hold value, a Second-Place Leader recognizes that humility, empathy, and a deep understanding of the human experience are equally crucial.

Unlike the conventional idea of leadership, which revolves around climbing a ladder to reach the pinnacle of success, the Second-Place Leader takes a different route. They understand that leadership is not a solo expedition but a collective journey. This journey demands the strength to confront one's limitations, the wisdom to seek guidance from others, and the courage to step aside when necessary.

Throughout this book, we will delve into the qualities that define the Second-Place Leader and explore how these characteristics can transform not only the leader but also those they lead. We will learn that true leadership lies not in the pursuit of a title or recognition but in the relentless pursuit of making a positive impact on the lives of others.

CHAPTER II

THE JOURNEY OF A SECOND-PLACE LEADER

Embracing Humility and Acknowledging Limitations

In the pursuit of leadership, humility is a trait that shines like a guiding star for the Second-Place Leader. Embracing humility means recognizing one's strengths and weaknesses, understanding that no leader is infallible, and acknowledging that growth comes from learning and openness to new perspectives.

The journey of a Second-Place Leader begins with a humble self-assessment, understanding that leadership is not about showcasing superiority or seeking personal glory. It is about serving a higher purpose, lifting others, and achieving collective success. By acknowledging limitations, a Second-Place Leader creates an environment where team members feel comfortable expressing their ideas and taking ownership of their roles.

Let's look at the story of my encounter with a former technology company where I worked. I was eager to fit in as a new employee when I first joined the organization. My strong academic background and problem-solving abilities originally made it difficult for me to ask for help or admit when I didn't have all the answers when I took the role of Manager of Field Operations (MOFO) in a promising technology business. This ego-driven strategy created conflict within the team, which hindered collaboration and stifled innovation.

However, my perspective shifted when I encountered a particularly challenging project that demanded expertise beyond my grasp. Instead of stubbornly pushing forward, I humbly sought guidance from a more experienced team member named Ed from another department. The result was remarkable; the team rallied together, and their combined efforts led to a breakthrough solution.

Embracing humility doesn't mean undermining one's capabilities but recognizing that true leadership is about empowering others and leveraging collective intelligence. A Second-Place Leader who embraces humility creates a culture where team members feel valued, respected, and motivated to contribute their best.

Building Trust and Fostering Strong Relationships

Trust is the foundation upon which every successful team is built, and a Second-Place Leader understands its significance. Building trust requires transparency, consistency, and genuine care for the well-being of team members. Trust is earned through actions that demonstrate reliability and credibility.

A Second-Place Leader must establish an open and supportive environment, where individuals feel safe to express their concerns, share their ideas, and make mistakes without fear of repercussions. Effective communication, active listening, and an unwavering commitment to the team's goals are essential aspects of building trust.

Let's look at the story of my wife Brenda, at the time she was promoted over her peers to the Manager of Human Resources at the Army & Air Force Exchange Service (AAFES) Europe located in Hanau, West Germany). Brenda took the time to build personal connections with her team members, showing genuine interest in their lives, aspirations, and challenges. She believed that understanding her team on a personal level would lead to better collaboration and higher performance.

Through her efforts, she not only built trust but also inspired loyalty among her team members. They knew she had their best interests at heart, and this deepened their commitment to achieving the organization's targets. The strong relationships she fostered within the team allowed for open dialogue and a culture of continuous improvement.

Balancing Ambition with Selflessness

Ambition is a powerful driving force that propels individuals to achieve greatness, but when left unchecked, it can overshadow the spirit of altruism. For a Second-Place Leader, the success of the team depends on finding a good balance between ambition with a genuine desire to help others.

The pursuit of personal goals should align with the greater vision of the organization or project. A Second-Place Leader's ambition is not solely self-serving; it is intertwined with the collective mission and the success of the leader and the team.

My youngest daughter, Tammy, is the Chief Executive Officer of RW Events, a business that plans weddings and other events. She is a good example of how ambition and kindness can go hand in hand. Tammy really wanted to grow her business and one day lead her own team. Still, she knew that for her to reach her goals, she had to first make a big difference in her company and the event planning industry.

With this mindset, Tammy wholeheartedly dedicated herself to supporting the organization's goals, going above and beyond to ensure its success. Her ambition helped her create a good work environment, give her team more power, and make the most of the organization's reach. As a result, she earned the respect of her employees, peers, and other leaders in her industry, and she became a role model for aspiring leaders who want to become entrepreneurs.

The Role of Empathy in Effective Leadership

Empathy is the heart of effective leadership, and it plays a crucial role in the journey of a Second-Place Leader. The ability to understand and relate to the emotions, challenges, and aspirations of team members creates a supportive and inclusive work environment.

Empathy enables a Second-Place Leader to offer genuine support, celebrate successes, and provide comfort during setbacks. It fosters strong bonds within the team and motivates individuals to perform at their best. A Second-Place Leader who practices empathy leads with compassion, inspiring others to do the same.

Take the example of Dr. Brian, who oversees operations at a non-profit organization. Dr. Brian has a natural ability to understand how his team members feel and what they are going through. He makes it a point to check in with them often, asking how they are doing and listens to them when they need it.

Dr. Brian plans team-building events and gives people ways to deal with stress when things are especially stressful. His caring attitude helps the team feel like a group, which makes them stronger and more committed to the organization.

As a Second-Place Leader, cultivating empathy ensures that decisions and actions are rooted in consideration for the team's collective needs, not just individual ambitions. It creates a sense of unity and purpose that empowers the team to overcome challenges together, leading to greater success in achieving shared goals.

CHAPTER III

LEADING BY EXAMPLE

How does a Second-Place Leader inspire and motivate others? By leading through actions, not just words. They understand that the most potent form of leadership comes from setting an example that others can look up to and emulate. This chapter explores the power of leading by example and how it can transform the dynamics within a team or organization.

The Power of Actions

As it has been said, actions speak louder than words. As a Second-Place Leader, your behavior and choices become a canvas on which others paint their perception of leadership. Your team members keenly observe how you tackle challenges, handle successes, and deal with failures. Your responses in critical situations become guiding lights for their own decision-making process.

If you demonstrate integrity and honesty in your dealings, your team will trust you more readily. If you are open to feedback and willing to admit your mistakes, your team will feel comfortable doing the same. If you show genuine care and appreciation for your team's efforts, they will reciprocate by going the extra mile.

Embracing Vulnerability

Leading by example doesn't mean being infallible. In fact, it's about acknowledging your vulnerabilities and using them to connect with your team on a human level. As a Second-Place Leader, you have the courage to show vulnerability, understanding that it cultivates an environment of trust and camaraderie.

Share stories of times when you faced challenges and what you learned from them. Be open about areas where you seek improvement and demonstrate how you actively work on self-development. This vulnerability not only humanizes you in the eyes of your team but also encourages them to embrace their own imperfections and strive for growth.

Empowering Others

Leading by example isn't just about showcasing your own abilities; it's about empowering others to reach their potential. A Second-Place Leader recognizes the strengths and talents of their team members and provides them with opportunities to shine.

Delegate responsibilities and trust your team to handle them with competence. Offer guidance and support when needed, but also step back and allow your team to take ownership of their projects. By empowering others, you instill a sense of ownership and pride, fostering a team of proactive individuals who contribute to collective success.

A Culture of Excellence

The influence of a Second-Place Leader extends beyond individual actions. It permeates the organization's culture and sets the bar for excellence. When you consistently strive for the highest standards and expect the same from your team, you create a culture of continuous improvement.

Celebrate achievements and recognize exceptional efforts, reinforcing the values and behaviors that drive success. A culture of excellence motivates team members to push their boundaries, elevating the collective performance to new heights.

In Summary

Leading by example is a core tenet of Second-Place Leadership. It is not about occupying a position of authority and expecting obedience; it is about inspiring and empowering others to become leaders. Your actions, vulnerabilities, and dedication to excellence will lay the foundation for a cohesive and high-performing team that values the well-being and growth of everyone.

CHAPTER IV
SERVANT LEADERSHIP

Servant Leadership is not just a management philosophy; it is a profound way of life that prioritizes the needs of others above self-interest. In the journey of a Second-Place Leader, embracing the principles of Servant Leadership can lead to transformative experiences, fostering a harmonious and highly productive work environment. (Robert K. Greenleaf)

The Concept of Servant Leadership

The concept of Servant Leadership has been around for centuries, but it was popularized by Robert K. Greenleaf in the 1970s. At its core, Servant Leadership challenges the traditional hierarchical approach to leadership and emphasizes the leader's responsibility to serve and support their team members.

A servant leader is not focused on accumulating power or achieving personal gain; instead, they seek to uplift, empower, and inspire those around them. This approach builds trust, enhances team morale, and promotes a sense of ownership and commitment among team members.

The Life-Changing Encounter

While already well-versed in leadership due to extensive military experience, leadership certifications, studying numerous books on the subject, and service in ministry, the true essence of Servant Leadership became crystal clear to me as the Second-Place Leader in a life-changing encounter.

Working under the guidance of Richard, the Chief Financial Officer and a remarkable leader, I served as the Director of Operations and believed I understood leadership comprehensively. However, Richard saw something in me and recognized an opportunity to elevate my understanding even further. One day, Richard pulled me aside and presented me with a book on Servant Leadership.

This single gesture proved to be a pivotal moment for me as the Director of Operations. The book merged the two things I already understood deeply—military leadership and ministry leadership—and combined them into one cohesive approach. I delved into the pages of the book with an open mind and a willingness to embrace a new perspective.

The Fusion of Military Leadership and Ministry

As the Director of Operations, I immersed myself in the principles of Servant Leadership, I discovered how it naturally aligned with my values and experiences. In the military, leadership had been about camaraderie, teamwork, and the mission's success. Similarly, in ministry, it had been about serving others, providing guidance, and fostering spiritual growth.

Servant Leadership took these two core principles—the selfless dedication to the mission and the genuine desire to serve others—and brought them together in a powerful and transformative way. As Director, I realized that a true leader is one who dedicates themselves to the betterment of the team, creating an environment where each member thrives and contributes their best.

The Impact on Leadership Style

Armed with this newfound understanding, I began implementing Servant Leadership principles into my daily interactions with the team. I listened more attentively to their needs, sought to understand their perspectives, and prioritized their growth and well-being.

I noticed that this shift in leadership style led to an incredible transformation within the team. Members felt valued, appreciated, and motivated to go above and beyond in their roles. The work environment became more positive, collaborative, and focused on achieving shared goals.

Furthermore, as the Director of Operations, I realized that Servant Leadership not only improved the department's performance but also contributed to my personal growth and fulfillment as a leader. The joy of seeing others succeed and thrive brought a profound sense of purpose and satisfaction.

Conclusion

The encounter with Servant Leadership profoundly impacted me, shaping my leadership philosophy in a way that integrated my military experience and ministry background. Embracing the principles of Servant Leadership allowed me to elevate my role as a Second-Place Leader, leading others for others, and making a lasting and positive impact on the team.

The story of Richard's gesture and the subsequent exploration of Servant Leadership underscores the transformative potential of this leadership style. By adopting Servant Leadership principles, Second-Place Leaders can create a culture of support, empowerment, inclusiveness, and growth, making their journey as leaders all the more meaningful and rewarding.

CHAPTER V

LEADING WITH PURPOSE

Identifying and Aligning Personal Values with Leadership Style

At the heart of leading with purpose lies the essential task of identifying and aligning personal values with one's leadership style. A Second-Place Leader must delve into their core beliefs, ethics, and principles to establish a strong foundation for their leadership journey.

Understanding personal values enables leaders to make consistent and authentic decisions, promoting trust and respect among team members. When values are aligned with leadership practices, the leader's actions become a reflection of their true self, inspiring others to follow their lead willingly.

John C. Maxwell emphasizes this crucial aspect of leadership, stating, "A leader is one who knows the way, goes the way, and shows the way." Identifying and aligning personal values sets the course for the leader, guiding them in navigating challenges and staying steadfast in their commitment to the team and its goals.

Setting Meaningful Goals and Objectives for the Team

Effective leadership is anchored in the ability to set meaningful and achievable goals and objectives for the team. A Second-Place Leader must take a collaborative approach, involving team members in the goal-setting process to encourage ownership and a shared sense of purpose.

Meaningful goals are not only outcome-oriented but also address the personal and professional growth of team members. As a leader, nurturing an environment where individual aspirations align with team goals empowers team members to invest their skills and passion wholeheartedly.

John C. Maxwell aptly encapsulates this aspect of leading with purpose, stating, "A leader is great not because of their power, but because of their ability to empower others." By setting meaningful goals, a Second-Place Leader empowers the team, creating a unified force working towards a common vision.

Using Leadership to Make a Positive Impact on the World

Beyond achieving organizational success, leading with purpose extends to making a positive impact on the world.

A Second-Place Leader must adopt a visionary outlook, seeking opportunities to contribute to the community, society, and the environment.

Leadership is not confined to the four walls of an organization; it is a catalyst for change and progress. By leveraging their influence, a Second-Place Leader can inspire others to embrace social responsibility, empathy, and sustainable practices.

In the words of John C. Maxwell, "Leadership is not about being in charge. It is about taking care of those in your charge." This sentiment aligns perfectly with the essence of leading with purpose. A Second-Place Leader, by using their influence to make a positive impact, empowers team members to blossom as change agents, united in their pursuit of a better future.

Conclusion

Leading with purpose requires a profound understanding of personal values, the art of setting meaningful goals, and a commitment to creating a positive impact on the world.

The journey of a Second-Place Leader is not merely about achieving success for themselves or their organization but about embracing a higher purpose.

By aligning personal values with leadership style, setting meaningful goals, and using leadership as a force for good, a Second-Place Leader leads with authenticity and inspires their team to greatness.

As a result, the impact of a Second-Place Leader reverberates far beyond their immediate sphere of influence. It resonates with the team, the organization, and the wider community, leaving a lasting legacy of positive change and empowerment.

CHAPTER VI

EMPOWERING OTHERS TO LEAD

Recognizing Potential in Others and Nurturing Their Talents

Empowering others to lead begins with recognizing the untapped potential within team members and nurturing their unique talents. A Second-Place Leader must adopt a keen sense of observation, understanding that everyone brings valuable skills and perspectives to the table.

By identifying individual strengths, a Second-Place Leader can assign tasks that align with team members' expertise, inspiring a sense of purpose and confidence. Cultivating a culture that values diversity and individual contributions fosters an environment where team members feel appreciated and motivated to excel.

Just like a gardener tends to each plant with care, a Second-Place Leader nurtures their team members, providing them with the support, training and development, and resources they need to flourish. As team members thrive and grow, the collective success of the team is elevated.

Delegating Effectively to Empower Team Members

Delegation is a cornerstone of empowering others to lead. A Second-Place Leader must master the art of assigning responsibilities according to team members' capabilities, trusting them to take ownership of their tasks. Effective delegation fosters a sense of autonomy and responsibility among team members.

Personal story about my dad and the philosophy of Macromanaging vs. Micromanaging:

Growing up with a father who owned multiple businesses taught me a valuable lesson about empowering others to lead. In his role as an entrepreneur, my dad faced the challenge of managing businesses across different towns, unable to be present at all of them simultaneously and not having fortune of the modern technology of today. This situation demanded a conscious decision about how he would oversee the operations.

My dad believed in empowering his managers and employees, giving them the autonomy to make decisions and manage their respective businesses. He adopted a macro management approach, focusing on the big picture, and trusting his teams to handle the day-to-day details.

He understood that micromanaging would stifle creativity, hinder growth, and create a sense of mistrust among his employees. Instead, he encouraged open communication and regular updates, allowing him to stay informed without being overbearing.

This philosophy of macro managing vs. micromanaging taught me that empowering others to lead involves giving them the space to make decisions, learn from their experiences, and grow as leaders themselves. As a Second-Place Leader, I apply this valuable lesson by delegating tasks to my team members, providing guidance and support when needed, but ultimately trusting them to excel in their roles.

Encouraging a Culture of Continuous Learning and Growth

Empowering others to lead can be an ongoing process that thrives in a culture of continuous learning and growth. A Second-Place Leader must encourage team members to seek personal and professional development, recognizing that investing in their growth benefits both the individual and the organization.

Promoting a culture of learning involves providing opportunities for skill development, training programs, and mentorship. As team members acquire new knowledge and skills, they become more capable leaders, ready to take on greater responsibilities and challenges.

A personal commitment to continuous learning sets an example for the team. As a Second-Place Leader, I strive to lead by example, attending workshops, seeking feedback, and continuously improving my own leadership skills. This approach stimulates a sense of shared growth and accountability within the team.

Conclusion

Empowering others to lead is not just about assigning tasks and responsibilities; it is about recognizing the potential in each team member, nurturing their talents, and trusting them to take ownership of their roles. Through effective delegation, a Second-Place Leader enables team members to thrive and flourish.

Drawing from my personal experience with my dad's philosophy of macro-management vs. micro-managing, I understand the importance of giving others the space to grow and develop as leaders. By cultivating a culture of continuous learning, a Second-

Place Leader creates a dynamic and empowered team, capable of achieving remarkable results.

In the journey of a Second-Place Leader, empowering others to lead becomes a guiding principle, transforming the team into a collective force of capable and motivated individuals.

CHAPTER VII

OVERCOMING OBSTACLES AND RESILIENCE

Strategies for Handling Setbacks and Challenges

In my experience, I have found that in the journey of a Second-Place Leader, obstacles and challenges are inevitable. However, the integration of faith in God and His word offers a unique and profound perspective on how to approach and overcome these hurdles. By anchoring our trust in a higher power, as a Second-Place Leader, I have gained strength and resilience in facing setbacks. This unwavering belief in divine guidance has been a source of encouragement and determination, guiding me through difficult times and empowering me to lead with conviction and grace.

Drawing inspiration from the wisdom found in Scripture, a Second-Place Leader learns valuable strategies for handling challenges. Scriptures often emphasize the importance of perseverance, seeking guidance through prayer, and trusting in God's plan. When facing adversity, a Second-Place Leader turns to these principles, finding hope, comfort, and guidance.

Developing Resilience as a Leader

Resilience is a vital trait for a Second-Place Leader, and faith in God can be a powerful source of resilience. Believing that challenges serve a greater purpose and that one is not alone in facing them encourages a steadfast mindset. A Second-Place Leader leans on their faith to develop the resilience needed to navigate through tough times.

As a leader, challenges may come in the form of organizational crises, unexpected changes, or personal setbacks. Embracing faith allows a Second-Place Leader to view these trials as opportunities for growth and refinement. With God's strength as their foundation, they can remain composed, adapt to new situations, and find solutions even amidst adversity.

Encouraging a Resilient and Adaptable Team

A Second-Place Leader plays a crucial role in shaping the team's response to challenges. By sharing their faith-driven resilience, they can inspire their team to embrace a similar perspective. Encouraging team members to draw on their faith, regardless of their individual beliefs, fosters a sense of unity and shared purpose in facing obstacles.

Openly expressing reliance on faith can also create an environment where team members feel comfortable discussing their struggles and seeking support. This openness further advances a culture of empathy and understanding, where team members can lean on each other for strength and encouragement.

In challenging times, a Second-Place Leader reminds their team that they are not alone but are part of a united effort. By infusing hope and trust in God's plan, they instill confidence in their team's ability to persevere, adapt, and overcome any obstacle that comes their way.

Conclusion

Integrating faith in God into the journey of a Second-Place Leader infuses the leadership approach with resilience, hope, and an unwavering belief in a higher purpose. Through prayer and reflection on Scripture, strategies for handling setbacks become deeply rooted in faith, guiding the leader in times of adversity.

Resilience is developed through trust in God's providence and the understanding that challenges are opportunities for growth and learning. A Second-Place Leader's faith-driven resilience empowers them to lead with confidence and grace, inspiring their team to face challenges with courage and determination.

By fostering an environment of shared faith and encouragement, a Second-Place Leader cultivates a team that embraces resilience and adaptability. As faith and leadership intertwine, obstacles become stepping stones to greater heights of success, unity, and shared purpose.

CHAPTER VIII

ETHICAL LEADERSHIP

The Importance of Integrity and Ethical Decision-Making

Ethical leadership is the cornerstone of a Second-Place Leader's character and influence. Upholding integrity and making ethical decisions are fundamental for establishing trust and credibility among team members. A Second-Place Leader must serve as a role model, demonstrating unwavering adherence to moral principles in their actions and decisions.

Integrity is the bedrock of ethical leadership, reflecting a leader's commitment to honesty, transparency, and accountability. By leading with integrity, a Second-Place Leader stimulates a culture of trust and respect within the team, enhancing collaboration and overall performance.

Addressing Ethical Dilemmas as a Leader

Ethical dilemmas are inevitable challenges that a Second-Place Leader may encounter. Addressing these dilemmas requires a steadfast commitment to ethical principles and the willingness to make difficult decisions with fairness and impartiality.

When faced with ethical dilemmas, a leader must carefully assess the potential consequences of various choices and consider the well-being of all stakeholders. By drawing from ethical principles, the leader can make decisions that align with their values and uphold the organization's reputation and values.

Upholding Moral Principles in the Face of Adversity

In times of adversity, a Second-Place Leader's commitment to ethical leadership is put to the test. External pressures or challenging circumstances should not compromise the leader's moral principles. Upholding integrity during difficult times reinforces the leader's credibility and strengthens the team's confidence.

Personal Story: Queena

An Exemplar of Ethical Leadership

One individual who embodies ethical leadership is Queena, my oldest daughter, and an aspiring attorney. Throughout her life, she has demonstrated a profound commitment to integrity and ethical practices. Even though she is not yet practicing law, the current demanding company she works for emphasizes the importance of attention to detail and doing things right the first time.

Queena's dedication to ethical leadership was evident from a young age. She insisted on being mindful of wasting energy, long before climate change awareness became widespread. Her sense of responsibility towards conserving resources was rooted in her belief in stewardship and caring for the environment.

As her father, I have always been mindful of the decisions I make and the way I operate around her. Her strong sense of integrity serves as a constant reminder to lead by example and uphold ethical standards in all aspects of life.

Queena's belief in following rules and going by the book reflects her commitment to fairness and justice. These qualities align seamlessly with her aspirations to become an attorney, where her ethical leadership will undoubtedly make a positive impact on her future clients and colleagues.

Conclusion

Ethical leadership is an essential aspect of a Second-Place Leader's journey, highlighting the significance of integrity, ethical decision-making, and upholding moral principles. By leading with honesty, transparency, and accountability, a Second-Place

Leader promotes a culture of trust and respect within their team.

Addressing ethical dilemmas requires a strong sense of responsibility and a commitment to making decisions that align with one's values and the welfare of all stakeholders. In the face of adversity, unwavering dedication to ethical principles reinforces the leader's credibility and inspires confidence in the team.

Queena's steadfast dedication to ethical leadership serves as a compelling example, highlighting the significance of ethical values and principles in leadership. Her story further emphasizes the importance of leading with integrity and ethics. As a Second-Place Leader, embracing ethical leadership enriches the journey, fostering a positive impact on

CHAPTER IX

LEADING FOR A BETTER FUTURE

The Impact of Second-Place Leaders on Society

Second-Place Leaders play a significant role in shaping society and influencing positive change. As a proud father of three sons, Landers, Dedrick, and Demedrick, I have witnessed the impact of their leadership and resilience in the face of challenges.

Each of my sons has faced their share of setbacks, yet they have demonstrated remarkable determination and resourcefulness, rising above adversity to achieve their own versions of success. Their experiences have shown me that Second-Place Leaders are not defined by their position but by their dedication to making a difference in the lives of others and their commitment to serving a greater purpose.

Encouraging a Collective Approach to Leadership

My sons' journeys have taught me the value of a collective approach to leadership.

While traditional leadership often emphasizes individual achievements, Second-Place Leaders recognize the importance of collaboration, support, and empowering others to reach their full potential.

Demedrick, the youngest of my sons, may no longer be with us, but his legacy of caring for others' lives on in the hearts of his friends and family. Despite his young age, he had a larger-than-life personality and a heart of gold. He exemplified the essence of a Second-Place Leader, caring for others, encouraging them to strive for a better future, and helping them accomplish their dreams.

Creating a Legacy that Outlasts Individual Achievements

Demedrick's impact on his friends and family exemplifies the essence of creating a legacy that outlasts individual achievements. While individual accomplishments are significant, a Second-Place

Leader understands that their true impact lies in the positive influence they have on others and the lasting change they inspire.

As a Second-Place Leader, my ultimate goal is to leave a legacy of empowerment, encouragement, and support for those around me. By investing in the growth and development of others, I can promote a culture of leadership that extends far beyond my own accomplishments.

Conclusion

The journey of a Second-Place Leader goes beyond individual achievements and positions of authority. Through the examples set by my sons and the legacy of caring left by Demedrick, I have come to understand the profound impact Second-Place Leaders can have on society.

Encouraging a collective approach to leadership, Second-Place Leaders understand that true success lies in empowering others and making a positive difference in their lives. By creating legacies that inspire, uplift, and support, Second-Place Leaders leave a lasting imprint on the world, one that continues to shape a better future for generations to come.

CHAPTER X

DEALING WITH UNFORESEEN CHALLENGES

Not Every Idea Receives Acceptance

As a Second-Place Leader, you must accept the fact that not every idea you suggest to the top leader will be accepted right away. Any organization or leadership situation can have complicated dynamics, and the top leader has their own goals, objectives, and concerns. Even though it can be frustrating, it's important to face these scenarios with a positive attitude and a willingness to learn.

The Saul and David Experience

When Resentment Arises

From what I've seen, being a Second-Place Leader can be like the story of Saul and David in the Bible. David was chosen to be the next king, but he worked for Saul, who was in charge at the time. Even though

David was always willing to help Saul, he ran into problems when Saul started to dislike his help and saw him as a threat to his own position.

In a similar way, you may find yourself in a situation where you support and help the top leader with all your heart, only to feel a hint of resentment. This Saul and David experience can be hard on your emotions because of how complicated your part is and how it might make you feel.

Dealing with Unforeseen Challenges

To get through these challenges as a Second-Place Leader, you have to stay true to your ideals and your mission. Learn to be strong, to be patient, and to accept God's plan. It is important to keep the lines of dialogue open and try to understand each other to create an atmosphere of mutual respect and cooperation.

Conclusion

As we learn more about what it's like to be a Second-Place Leader, we know that not every idea will be accepted right away. You will be able to get through tough times if you embrace resilience and stay committed to working with integrity.

The story of Saul and David is a powerful warning of how complicated it is to be a leader. If you have to deal with anger or unexpected problems, do it with kindness and humility. Stay true to your commitment to a higher cause and your role as a Second-Place Leader. Have faith that your efforts are part of God's bigger plan.

CHAPTER XI

CONCLUSION

In the journey of a Second-Place Leader, we have explored various aspects of leadership that go beyond traditional notions of authority and position. Throughout this book, we have emphasized the importance of embracing Second-Place Leadership and leading for the benefit of others. Here are the key points and lessons we have learned:

1. Second-Place Leaders are essential supporters: In the realm of leadership, the focus is often on the top leader, but Second-Place Leaders play a crucial role in supporting, executing, and realizing the vision of the top leader.
2. Leading with humility and recognizing limitations: Second-Place Leaders acknowledge their strengths and weaknesses, understanding that true leadership involves

humility and a willingness to learn from others.

3. Empowering others to lead: A central tenet of Second-Place Leadership is empowering team members to thrive and take ownership of their roles, fostering a culture of continuous learning and growth.
4. Ethical leadership and integrity: Upholding moral principles is fundamental in navigating ethical dilemmas and challenges, leading with transparency and accountability.
5. Creating a legacy beyond individual achievements: The impact of Second-Place Leadership goes beyond individual accomplishments, leaving a lasting legacy of empowerment, encouragement, and support for others.

Embracing Second-Place Leadership is not a compromise but a choice to make a lasting impact on the lives of others. Throughout this book, we have seen how Second-Place Leaders can bring positive change to their teams, organizations, and communities. By recognizing the value of supporting the top leader and empowering others, readers can embrace their unique position and contribute to a stronger and more cohesive leadership culture.

Remember, leadership is not limited to titles or positions of authority. Anyone can be a Second-Place Leader and make a significant difference in the lives of those around them. By embracing Second-Place Leadership, readers can unlock their full potential as leaders and create a positive and lasting impact on the world.

The essence of Second-Place Leadership lies in leading for the benefit of others. A leader's purpose should be rooted in serving, supporting, and empowering those we lead. By leading with compassion, empathy, and a genuine desire to help others succeed, we create an environment of trust and collaboration that breeds success and fulfillment.

As you embark on your leadership journey, remember the words of John C. Maxwell, "Those closest to the leader will determine the success level of that leader." The impact of a Second-Place Leader ripples through the lives of those they support, uplift, and empower. By focusing on the well-being and growth of others, we can foster a community of leaders dedicated to making a positive difference.

"Second-Place Leader: Leading Others for Others" has explored the essence of Second-Place Leadership and its profound impact on individuals and society. As we conclude this journey, let us embrace the role of supporting the top leader, empowering others to lead, and leading with integrity and compassion. Let us create legacies of empowerment and encouragement, leaving a lasting imprint on the world.

By adopting Second-Place Leadership, we can collectively contribute to a future where leadership is not confined to titles but driven by a genuine desire to benefit others. As you continue your leadership path, remember that the mark of a true leader lies in the positive influence they have on others and the legacy they leave behind.

May this book inspire you to embrace your role as a Second-Place Leader and lead for the benefit of others, creating a better and more compassionate world for generations to come.

"As you reach the end of this book, I want to offer you something special. If you've enjoyed the journey so far and want to continue exploring this world or stay updated on my future works, simply scan the QR code below or visit our website at www.authorwebsite.com."

Instructions:

To access the exclusive content, promotions, and updates, simply use your smartphone or tablet to scan the QR code above. You'll be directed to a page where you can subscribe to our newsletter, join our Facebook group, and receive a free short story set in the same universe as this book.

Thank you for being a part of this literary adventure, and I look forward to sharing more books with you in the future!

REFERENCES

1. Maxwell, John C. Developing the Leaders Around You. HarperCollins Leadership, 1995.
2. Maxwell, John C. The 21 Irrefutable Laws of Leadership,. Harper Collins Leadership,1998 and 2007.
3. Greenleaf, Robert K. Wikipedia. https://en.wikipedia.org/wiki/Servant_leadership #.
4. Maxwell, John C. https://blog.leadr.com/5-leadership,

www.ingramcontent.com/pod-product-compliance
Lightning Source LLC
La Vergne TN
LVHW020513100826
845148LV00003B/772

* 9 7 9 8 9 8 5 9 7 1 3 5 4 *